Sweet Tea and Ketamine

Also by Zeinab Fakih

I Didn't Know How To Say This. So, I Wrote It Down

Sweet Tea and Ketamine

By Zeinab Fakih

Sweet Tea and Ketamine copyright © 2021 by Zeinab Fakih. All rights reserved. No part of this book may be used or reproduced in any manner whatsoever without written permission except in the case of reprints in the context of reviews.

ISBN: 978-1-7777268-1-2

Cover: Nour Aljumaa

Tragedies

You're a tragedy
I'd die for any day.

Care for an adventure?

Let's run to forever.
Second star to the right
and straight on until morning.
Keep going and never turn back.
Like how Romeo and Juliet should have ended.
We could see what should have happened
if Gatsby had just said yes to leaving with Daisy.
We can be the good endings to the love stories that failed.
We can be their happily ever after.
So, meet me under the old oak tree
at the stroke of midnight
and let's disappear.

Mizpah

Anticipate a red flush,
an incandescent heart rush.
Velvet words of candor
you walk around like folklore.
A mythical creature.
Temptations fall
close to rapport.
Stirring the lights
of your ghosts.
Your Midas touch
like galore.
Sweet tea mixed with your voice
but I would rather be alone.

Ketamine

Intoxicated with madness.
Consumed with sadness.
Infatuated with misery.
Captivated by heartache.
Stimulated by sorrow.
And high on bleakness.

First Time

Do you believe in that whole
first-time, love-at-first-site kind of feeling?
Do you believe in fate?
That two people were meant to meet at an exact moment.
Do you believe in destiny?
Because I didn't think I did.
Not until I met you.
Because people like you don't just randomly meet people like me.
You are too perfect.
You are too unlike anyone else I know.
It's like you were the pieces I fell for in other people all wrapped up in one person.
But if I'm not that for you,
and if you don't really believe in all that
then I feel pretty stupid right now.
But I think you do.

Nervous

The butterflies in my stomach have gone on a rampage.
My mind is cloudy.
My knees are weak.
I can feel my heartbeat quicken as we make eye contact.
It's like my body is physically linked to you.
As though it senses when you're nearby.
Like your presence shuts me down.
But I kind of like it.

Didn't think people like you still existed.

I thought you were so corny
the way you'd call me pretty
and compliment me in cliches.
But you'd defend yourself
and claim that, sometimes, the truth is corny
and full of cliches.
I didn't know if I agreed or not.
I wanted too, though.
But then you said something that stunned me
and made me stare in awe
and I thought, maybe you'll be alright.

"The truth is like poetry.
And most people fucking hate poetry."

And even though we don't talk anymore-
and even though you probably don't remember me-
I hope you find the muse and create poetry.

The Secret History

The secret history
of you and I
lies in the bookshelves
under the letter "y."

Our story begins
in playlists made
full of words
we dare not relay.

We begin
in a polaroid lens.
The picture came out grey
but you kept it in your wallet.

A manifesto
of secret smiles
and stains of ink.
Laying on a couch
in an April spring.

To be was never a question.
All I knew
in the end would be true
was you and me.
Until our death is due.

Up 'til 3am

Because I've been keeping myself up until 3am every night
just to hear what you have to say.
Because I've been listening to music I would usually hate
but somehow really like
when you're the one recommending them.
Because I get so excited when you're out with friends
but still ask me to text you
because you don't want the conversation to end.
Because of those "how are you" texts
that you don't have to send.
Because I get so happy when you like a song I show you.
Because you don't say some cheesy line.
Because none of what you're saying makes sense
and you're tired
but you stay up 'til 3am.

Something about you

I don't usually do this
but you struck me in the right way.
And all of a sudden,
I had no control.

Dance with me

I want to sip water
while you sip champagne
as we celebrate.
I want to play an old record at 2am
and dance with you in the kitchen.
I want to bake cakes with you and wipe the chocolate
off your face.
I want to watch a new show
and eat all the food we could find.
I want to try that strange new restaurant with you.
I want to do all this with you and more.
I just want to dance through life
with you.

You Are My Home

He's hot coffee on a cold autumn morning.
He's the blanket you crawl under on a cozy, winter night.
He's the sound of calmness in a still, spring day.
He's the salty air as the sun sets in summer.
He's the seasons,
the weather,
my comfort,
my world.

He's what I need to get through another day.
He's what I hope to have every other day.
He brings me a warmth that a hot coffee can't.
He brings me a comfort that my blanket can't.
He brings me the serenity that stillness can't.
He brings me more joy than the seas could ever dream to.
He's more than the seasons,
the weather,
the comfort,
the world.

Blank

I've lost all words I used to write.
I spend my days staring at the blank page
that is my mind.
I've hit a writer's block in every aspect
of my life.
My days have become those few seconds after you
wake up and you are at a loss of what is happening.
It's waiting for the subway at 5am
and you're the only one there.
It's someone asking what's on your mind when,
all of a sudden, nothing is.
It's you telling me you love me
and me realizing,
that the white noise machine I've had residing in my
head?
The blur and the rush in my mind?
Has been me processing,
realizing,
and finding out
that I am madly in love with you.
And it scares me.
It makes my mind go numb.
It makes my senses fuzz.
And I am ready to jump right in,
and fall even further
in love with you.

What I Want

I want to wear your hoodie.
I want to fall asleep listening to your heartbeat
and wake up with your arms around me.
I want to play with your hair.
I want you to sing me to sleep.
I want to tell you everything about me.
I want you to kiss me softly.
I want to know every thought going through your head.
I want to tell you how I feel about you.
I want to tell you just how much I love you.
But I can't.
So, I'll just sit here breaking my own heart.

Do You Like Me?

Wish I was like the girls
in my mom's magazines.
Blonde hair draped around
on grass so green.
Muted tones fit more adequately.
Maybe then the boys would like me.

Wish I was one of those
pretty-in-pink, ivory.
Rosy cheeks on a rounded face
answer to the call of Emily.
Maybe if I would fit a bit more canonically
maybe then I'd be pretty.

Raise up the saturation.
Lower my expectations.
Change the way that my tongue sits
in a fuller mouth
adorned with pink lipstick.

Maybe if I cut my nails,
grew my hair,
and sat out of the sun.
Maybe if I changed my style,
removed my eyeliner,
was a little more "fun."
Maybe if I stopped carrying the weight of it all.
Maybe then
people might like me.

I Choose You.

I choose you.
I choose
the fact that we have totally different tastes in movies.
I choose you preferring sweet over savoury.
I choose the fact that
you're a night owl and I'm an up-at-5am person.
I choose you opting for tea over coffee.
I choose you pulling at your hair when you're
nervous.
I choose how you somehow understand stocks.
I choose your minimal risk to my insanity.
I choose you hating the snow.
I choose your weird friends.
I never know what your friends are talking about.
I choose you being a reckless driver.
I *choose* you.
I choose *you.*
I choose you.

Van Gogh's Got Nothing on You

He looked like art.
It was disarming but beautiful.
When you look at him it's as though
you see the world with new eyes.
Everything clears
but is also a million times harder to understand.
It's like he was painted with the best pigments,
using the best brushes.
As though he was carved
from the richest marble.
And I'm stunned
and completely floored by the fact
that I am so lucky
to be living here
at the same moment as you.

Meet me at the overpass.

You don't know
that every night
I sneak away and drive to the lookout
and I park at the end of the lot
before walking to the furthest side of the cliff.
Here, I see every light in this city
but I can't hear a single sound.
I am the eyes of Doctor T.J. Eckleburg
breathing in every light.
Looking up at the blackened sky
as my lungs fill with the air
between two stars.
Encapsulated by beauty.
Engrossed with tranquility.
And know that with each look you give
I am filled with more hope
than what all the stars in the galaxy could provide.

Shine for You

Oh, how the sun makes your green eyes shine.
As though it rose just for you.
As though it shines
just for the chance to hit your golden skin
and leave you glistening and warm.
Shining down on the flowers that bloom for you.
With each step you take
they bloom brighter, growing higher
yearning to brush up against you
and feel your touch
just hoping you'll notice their beauty.
Oh, how the earth goes on for you--
revolves for you.
So, you can feel the sun
and bathe in the light of the moon.
And how we are all alive for you.

truly, madly, deeply

I am truly, madly deeply, helplessly in love with you. Somehow you broke my walls down enough to render myself to you completely. And as you hold my heart in your hands, I ask that you not drop it. And as you explore my ruins, I ask that you not tell another soul of the hidden treasures I keep. And most of all, I ask that you do not give me a reason to rebuild with a new lock and banish you from my kingdom.

They asked me about love.

I love the way he says "thanks" while looking down.
As though he's too shy to really thank you.
I love the way he nods his head while listening
to the song that I hate so much.
I love the way he laughed when he took me out to sushi
and I ordered fries instead.
I hate him so much.
But I love him even more.
In the ways it counts.

Up at Night

I want to be the thing that keeps you up at night.
I want to be the person you can't stop thinking about.
I want you to keep your phone next to your bed,
hoping I call or text.
I want to be the person you wake up wanting to see.
I want to be the reason you're tossing and turning;
waiting to see.
I want our friends to tease us about how in love we are.
I just want to be the thing that keeps you up at night.

How don't you know?

You're so stupidly perfect.
I think you may be worth it–
giving all my time
and all my energy to.
Only you.
Want you to come over.
I'll gladly give it over.
Tie my hands behind my back.
Let you take over
all control.
And though we
have never met in person,
I still think you're worth it.
Pull back the curtains
of your soul.
Take over my own.

Since We Were Kids

I have loved you
since we were twelve years old.
Playing outside in the snow.
You'd hug me tight to keep me warm.

I have loved you
since we were sixteen.
Sneaking out
running through the street.
Last time we felt truly free.

I have loved you
since we were eighteen.
Our final year–
what a dream.
That's when you finally kissed me.

I still love you
now at 23.
You stand up in a suit
waiting for someone who isn't me.

I will still love you
until we're 65.
Though we may have different lives.
Just know
I'll always stand by your side.

And though you
haven't loved me

since we were twelve years old,
I'll still hold you tight.
Won't let go.
Take care of your sweetheart
and tell her she's your true love.

Can we try again?

Because I'm sitting in bed
with a huge lump in my throat
pulling and ripping the hair from my head
just to feel something.

A Play Worthy Kind of Love

Read me old sonnets and words of love
Put Shakespeare to shame with how in love we are,
with how far we'd go for each other.
Because I'd go to the end of the world for you.
Just say the word and I'm off
"How high"
      when you tell me to jump.
"How fast"
      when you tell me to run.
"How long"
      when you tell me to wait.
For to be a glove on the hand that rests on your cheek
would mean the world to me.

I Like Me Better with You

"Your worth is not measured by who you're with"
I know.
"You are strong and independent"
I am.
"You do not need a man to tell you you're pretty"
I agree.
"You are smart"
I am.
I know all these things.
I'm pretty.
I'm smart,
I'm strong.
I'm independent.
I'm amazing.
I know these things.
But for some reason,
these words just sound better coming out of your mouth.
Because, with you
my mind shines
And my face glows.
I'm stronger
I'm greater.
And I guess I'm just better with you.

exhale

Heart skipping every other beat
I think I might die
there's a shaking in my hands
but not the respectful kind
the butterflies in my stomach
made room for the roaches
I wish my throat would open up
let me let out a cry
can I exhale the shakiness
and breathe in your "alright"
can I stop my knees from buckling
under the weight of my life
can I slow down this time
stop the room from spinning
can I let out a sigh
can relief reach my burning eyes
grip on the wall
maybe the bricks won't let me fall
heart on the floor
soaked through with mud and snow
I can't hear a thought
though I'm having them all
racing through my mind
can't pick one to hold
someone tell my lungs
stop filling with tar
someone tell my heart
stop exploding through the walls
of my compressing chest
collapsing on my bones

someone please tell my mind
the danger has to go
and peel my nails out of the crescents
they've imprinted in my palms

Roses are red, Vol. 1

You are a rose
and I love you
thorns and all.

Roses are red, Vol. 2

Roses are red
just like the bruise
you give to me at night
when I won't love you.

He

I know a boy,
who calls me crazy like it's a compliment.
Who drives a hundred miles per second.
Who likes to live his life like it's the end.
He's always racing.

And I know a boy,
who can't keep a single promise made.
Who can't sit still through standstill days.
Who likes the look of a mess to create.
He's always changing.

And we run away
to a great escape.
We pack our bags and change our names.
We say goodbye
to things left behind.
And we don't look back for a second.

I know a boy,
who brings out my smile like no one else.
He makes me laugh until I lose my breath.
And when I look at him I know for a fact,
I'm falling fast...

My Favourite Virus

It hurts.
It's loud.
It's sudden.
It seeps its way into your soul unexpectedly.

It leaves you scarred.
It leaves you scared.
You feel alone
yet full.

You're drowning
and you can't wait to sink down.
It's a virus.
The best one you can get.

Back to November

Eyes bright blue
or they could've been brown.
Can't remember.
So many days have passed since last November.
Freckles on your face.
They looked like constellations.
Wait, no, that's wrong.
Must've been my imagination.
Brown hair
or it could've been red.
Doesn't matter.
Either way this bed has no more laughter.
Sleeping alone
in a deafening city.
Got used to you
experiencing it with me.
That t-shirt you wore
on our very first date
still sits in my drawer.
A reminder of my favourite mistake
that just didn't take.
Eyes brown
or they could've been amber.
Doesn't matter now.
We've reached next November.

Hey...

I look for you in strangers faces.
I look for your deep brown eyes.
The way your head tilts back when you laugh.
The way you tap your fingers against your leg when you think.
I'm sad when I don't find you.
Even worse when I do.

Solstice

Under the twinkling lights,
your eyes like Tennessee sweet tea
on a Sunday afternoon
caught in an August rain
outshining them all.
Lay in the field of violets,
sought an aurora-filled sad note.
I'll paint this town blue.
Can't wait to forget you
as the leaves die beneath our feet
and we wash the sand away
under a blue-tinted glow.
Filter out the golden hues,
you look best in icy tones.
Eat the peaches
bruised from the fall
as our longest day ends
and it begins to snow.

Fairy Lights

I don't know what it is about winter.
Maybe it's the snow covering the streets like a soft blanket.
Maybe it's the lights
twinkling.
As though Tinkerbell herself lit the world.
Maybe it's forgetting gloves and having to walk
while holding hands just so we don't freeze.
Maybe it's standing close together
because the cold keeps me from speaking above a whisper.
Maybe it's sitting with everyone you love
under a warm blanket
by a warm fire
watching Christmas movies until you all fall asleep.
Maybe it's the holidays themselves.

Darkest Winter

You were a harsh blizzard.
You were slipping on black ice.
You were boots ruined from rock salt.
You were the sleet staining my pants.
You were the late sunrise and early sunset;
leaving me in dark day.
You were strong winds stinging my cheeks.
You were numb fingers and chapped lips.
But I still wanted to stand under the mistletoe;
kiss you a happy new year;
and be your Valentine;
no matter what.

It's the most wonderful time of the year

Lying in bed alone.
It is nearly reaching 4
am. Another list of uncommunicative men.
How many times can I answer the question,
"did it hurt when you fell from heaven?"

He asks me to kiss him underneath
the mistletoe
at his next party.
I agree even though I can't
tell which one is he
in his group of ten.

Go ahead and leave me with nothing
but a story to tell at the next luncheon:
You'll never believe what he texted
at 3am.
It's 4 o'clock in the morning.
Why does he think I'll be answering
"What are you up to tonight?"

Lying in bed
Making New Year's plans.
Writing my list
of resolutions:
Stop meeting boys under the mistletoe
whom you'll kiss just until you're sober.
And in your dreams, replace his face.
Confuse him with all of your past mistakes.

He said I looked like a rose
though he used the wrong "you're"
before explaining his intelligence,
drinking down false intellect.
"You look best in red,"
he says the first night we met.
"Sure," I say.
"By the way,
what is your name?"

'Tis the season
of grief-filled romance.
Maybe chivalry really is dead.
You can call me babe for the night
before inevitably blocking me
on the way to my flight.

'Tis the season
of half-filled truths.
One night only,
say I love you
like you have to all my roommates.
I can now tell you
how each of their lips taste
as we compare your texts
down to the identical comma.

Meet me under the mistletoe
by the back of the school gym.
Replay the same Christmas song.
Replay the same sin.
Turns out validation is my vice

and you're the punishment.
I must pay the price.

92 Johnson Avenue

It was the best of times,
the worst of nights.
Faded lights in a darkened room.
A too-gauche party,
that is, until she met you.
Took a dreary path
under a snowy sky
she was a fan, so she thought she'd try.
Forgot to stop and think it through.
Helped form the grip around
his Old-Fashioned love affair.
Clandestine meetings turned
"I do."

Scarlett letters tucked
deep in her favourite jacket
walking along
would-be Honeymoon Avenue.
But the honeymoon's over,
he whispered coming closer.
A peaceful ruler
could be the answer.
Could catch us in the downfall.

Queen of Hearts had other plans,
chopped off his head,
put him to rest
deep in the hill
dedicated to infidelity.
Clandestine meeting

turned illicit affairs
but I guess that's what happens
when you're too young to care.
The snow was magical,
she pleaded to the void-filled air.

Honeymoon Avenue
fixed with cobblestones
of ill-tempted fate.
I guess there was no use running
from a kingdom meant to come undone.
Maybe catching fire could help
relight the spark lost.
Who would've guessed,
he'd supply the match.

Lily

So, darling,
put your lips
next to mine.
We could lie
with the leaves.

Hold your
hand in mine
like the roots
of the trees.

You could
block out the sun
we don't need it
any longer.

So darling lay
still next to me.
Maybe we could
stop for a moment.

You asked me what my problem was...

My problem is the fact that I'm so crazy,
head over heels,
can't eat,
can't sleep,
in love with you.
But I can't find it in me to tell you.
Because you don't see me that way.
And I don't want to hurt you;
I don't want to ruin a perfect friendship.
I'm scared.
And it's selfish, I know.
But I can't bring it in me
to tell you the truth.

Miss You

Miss how you'd wake up in the night
droning on incessantly
about a dream where you died
and came back to haunt this city.
Miss the space between your eyes
where the stars would reside.
And the chip in your tooth
only showing up when you laugh.
And I miss the way you held my hand
and how you'd swing it beside you
as we ran on adventures.
Miss you asking me to close my eyes
and surprising me with your "I do."
When you dropped to your knee
and asked me "please?"
as the sun set behind you,
I knew it was meant to be.
Then you'd stare out the window forever more
but say nothing was wrong.
So, I picked up my pen
and wrote you a poem
to be said at your next wedding.
I hope you love her more.
I'll be waiting in my apartment
if you want to come to the door
or give me a call.
I wonder how you are.
You packed up so quickly and left so fast,
almost forgot your guitar.
The one that I gave you

on your 21st birthday
when you told me you loved me
and asked me to run away
and I said: I do.

I just thought you would too.

Your Weather Report

I thought you were sunshine
but then you came pouring in.
Thought you were a rainbow
but you hit me with lightning.
I like to swim
but your flood was too strong.
I love the snow
but your snowflakes turned into an ice storm.
The beach is so much fun
but you buried me alive in sand.
And every time
as I came out
bloodstained,
sore,
ready to quit,
you told me you love me
and I melted at your words.

'tis the season

The lights of the city are dimmed next to your glow.
The disco balls came from Sir Brummagem's shop next door.
I know I should control my idle hands. Alternate my messy plans. Delete your number.
Instead, I said, "what's one more mistake in a small town?"

I trip over the ice skates you bought me at sixteen.
They still fit like the warm gloves you held my face with.
Though the laces are left unclean.

Meet me at our spot by our favourite tree by the unkept mound.
What's another mistake in our small town?

Melt the ice, watch them drop.
Kiss me twice.
Kiss me before the inevitable halt of a Hallmark film.
The baker must go back to the big city.
Goodbye to the schoolteacher who taught her what Christmas is for.

Don't love you but I can't be alone right now

Brown skin turned golden from the day we spent at
the beach, on the sand. We couldn't move.
Instead, we stared up at the sky and counted the
clouds rolling by.
I counted seven you got thirteen.
But that's not surprising.
I spent most of my time counting the freckles on your
shoulders.
We got back home, and I put on my red dress. The one
I wore on our first date-
or so you say.
Either way, I know it's your favourite.
And you brushed your thumb along my cheek and
asked me, "dear, will you marry me?"
I shook my head no but spoke out a "yes" because I
wanted you to leave
but not quite yet.
So, you put a ring on my finger, and we laid in bed. On
your chest I rested my head.
I heard your heartbeat; it wasn't one filled with
excitement.
It was steady.
It was sure.
Like you knew what was coming.
And so that night, as the sun set, you took back your
ring and planted a kiss on my forehead.
You walked out the door and I knew
I'd never hear from you again,
and that was fine.

Because even though you're still on my mind, it's a soft memory of a day at the beach where you said you loved me
and that was complete.
We didn't need to continue because we didn't have anything.
But I still trace the mark where you placed your ring.
And curse the day I didn't say, "okay."

u up?

I remember lying in bed
that September night
wondering why you changed your mind.
You spent the day flirting
calling me cute
nicknamed me your baby
Oh, how sweet
But then you disappeared.
Texts went unanswered.
Message deleted.
It's like you forgot
the girl you were just appeasing.
Put on an old album,
play it on repeat
Listen to a girl song about a heartbreak
on Cornelia Street
And I can't help but think,
I shouldn't be this dramatic.
After all, it's not that romantic.

It's not like we dated.
We only ever held hands.

Not like we dated.
We only made empty plans.

You Only ever walked me to every class
and asked me to text you
to make sure I got home safe.
Gave me sunflowers

on Valentine's Day.

And I remember that late October night
as I rolled out of bed
for the hundredth time
and I saw a text
asking if I was still up
and I told you yes
and we talked in the phone until sunrise.
You said how wild it'd be if we dated, baby.
You said, "you're my best friend."
Ended with "I love you,
call me later today."

Again, it's not like we dated.

Miss Misfortune

Miss the nape of your neck.
Miss the games you played.
Miss the I love you's.
Miss the charade.
Miss the small talks.
Turned to deep talks.
Turned to long walks.
Turned to late nights,
missing your flight.
Turned to long hauls.
Miss the missed calls.
Never texted me back.
Missed the blocked messages.
Miss how you kissed
my strawberry lipstick.
Miss the mistrust.
Miss the fallout,
how I'd callout
but you'd ignore.
Left me on the dirty floor.

Hades

Let's run to a
dicranum-printed home
sat by Wordsworth.
Pray to Persephone
and bury ourselves
in cinnamon-scented solace
as we eulogize
our past lives.

Crow

Birds crash
against my window
every once in a while.
You'd think they'd see
how their friends fall.
Is it a bad omen?
Or is it me?
An instability of my aura?
An imbalance in my chakras?
One piece of me
is not like the other.
The problem is
I'm colour blind
so, they all look the same.
My window's now unhinged.
Paint chipped at the corners
from birds trying to break in
my quiet solace.

you asked me not to be scared

You brushed your finger
across my cheek.
Barely touching me
as though I would break.
And I could have.

I froze in disbelief
as you continued tracing
from my cheek down to my chin.
You held me like a flower.
Careful so my petals don't wilt.

And, finally, you grazed
my lips so gently
before planting a soft kiss
careful not to shatter me.

Prince of Hell

Hell was the journey
but it brought me to you.
Cold was the shoulder
enchanted by a blue hue.
Graced by your body
dancing in the shadows.
Stretch high to meet your eye
standing on my tiptoes.
Blood splattered, battered ram
crawling through the dirt.
Mud-stained glass
ripped through your white linen shirt.
Choked by the scarf
you gave me that night.
As you stared, tongue tied
trying to meet my eyes.
Ring my blood-slacked clothes
out with my tears.
Drown myself in an iced-down bath
as I remember the night that you said:

I'd love to rule with you
that would be amazing.
Mark my clay flesh
with your red lips grazing.
And time and time you'll show me again
what it's like to be a true ruler in hell.
Told me Aphrodite blessed our unity.
That your golden words were true to me.
We could dance by the fireside

hold my hand straight through the night.
And your fears will be obsolete
because even the false god
would bless this unity.

Calling Aphrodite

I hate Shakespeare
and Nicholas doesn't give me Sparks.
If hearts really skipped
we'd surely be gone.
I hate holding hands
or confiding in the dark.
Don't look for your face
in every parking lot.
Kissing in the rain
is a broken cliche.
And sometimes the bad boy
just can't be saved.
Eyes don't sparkle
when you lean in for a kiss.
Nights with you
are like the nights you miss.
Can't dance in the kitchen.
Our walls are too thin
and the neighbours hate it
so, we just stand still.
I can feel the silence
deep in my soul.
Warming the hands
I won't let you hold.

He looks as pretty as the Devil

Screaming and crying
Dancing' while we're dying
Stumbling into the bathroom stall.
Smoking in the driveway
Emotions flash like lightning.
What doesn't kill me
only makes me want you that much more.

Tuck me into a bed of nails
sing me to a nightmare ward.

And lift me up
smoke me out
burn me into a pile of ash.
Bleed me out.
Kill me now.
Wear my broken heart like a crown.

Surprise me staying idle
but choke me while you smile.

Shoot me between the eyes
and laugh as I die.

Cecilia

Sunday morning
you asked me to dance.
Played the song of death
while you spun me around the kitchen.
I grazed my hand on the marble topped island
and cut myself on broken glass.
Your white shirt now stained red.
As you stared in my eyes
without looking at me.
I was your blood-soaked beauty queen
And you were okay with that.
You were the crow tapping our window
trying to get in.
Floating in our minds.
Spinning me around
to the tune of a funeral
and I smiled as you buried me
into the weed-filled ground.

Wish you would

I wish you would come back,
wish I'd never said the things that I did.
Wish you would turn that car around
and come knock at my door.
Wish you were right here,
right now.
Wish you would apologize
but you're never one to call the first time.
Wish you would tell me
how you felt that very first night.
Wish I never
let you hold me and see me cry.
Wish I could erase
all our time.
Tell myself it's okay-
alright-
but you were never one for lies.

Reboot

I wish I could forget all about you.
I wish I could forget what it felt like to be with you.
To wake up next to you.
To have you tell me it's all going to be okay.
I want to forget how warm your smile made me feel.
I want to forget your laugh.
Your beautiful laugh.
I want to wake up having forgotten all about you.
I wish I could forget everything you've ever told me.
How you and your father can never agree on anything.
How your mom is your hero.
How you wish you were born somewhere else.
How you can sometimes resent your brother.
Everything.
I want to forget your existence.
I want to forget what you put me through.
I want to forget everything.

Climate change

It's like I'm happy during the day.
I'm just fine.
But when the sun sets,
the feelings arise.
All I want to do
is be right there beside you.
It's like a tidal wave.
You're a hurricane.
I'm broken and soaked.
Yet all I want to do
is swim in your whirlpool.
I might just sink
and possibly drown
but it's got to be better
than the feelings I've found
to fill the empty space
where your head used to lay.
It's like I'm finding myself,
I'm calling my friends.
I'm watching old shows
because I know how they end.
Still, all I want to do
is sink in the waves of your climate change.

Legend Says

And the story goes:
>I miss you but I know I shouldn't.
>And I hate how you mean something to me.
>And I wish I didn't care
>whether or not you had the decency
>to text me today.

And the story goes:
>Once upon a time,
>a girl reached out to a boy
>who hurt her some time ago.
>A whisper in her mind said,
>"leave it all alone.
>The past is a boy gone.
>Didn't rewrite it as before."
>But she still sent the letter
>attached to the claw of a crow.
>The ghost boy walking alone in exile
>seems to run through her brain.
>The ghost even the strongest coven
>can't seem to wash away with sage.
>He's running around
>hidden behind the shadows,
>a set of ruins they call a home.
>Though she scrubs it clean,
>she still finds him here.

And the story goes:
>Long ago,
>in a far-off land,

true love broke the curse.
But how do you break a spell
when the one you love
doesn't love you back?

eulogize me to the songs of Sinatra

If I keep replaying unsaid conversations
imagined in my head,
do you think we could have them one day?
If I memorize the lives
I've created for us
could you rehearse them and perform one tonight?
If I keep writing your name
in each notebook's empty space
do you think you could keep mine in your head
and maybe with each stroke of my pen
time won't erase me from your memory.
All the he-said
and the she-said
disappear from my head
and I'm stuck contemplating the question
of why I ever left.

Remind me why I left

Can no longer tell just what I saw
in the man with the brown eyes
who called me his all.
Was it the tattoo gracing his neck?
The one my fingers lingered on
as we lay in bed?

Or was it the rings
he adorned every day.
The ones who caused a comforting chill
as he wiped my tears away.

Was it how tall he stood?
Towering over me,
keeping the rain from drowning me.

Maybe it was his smile.
The one that would form against my lips
whenever he'd lean in
and ask for just one more kiss.

So, it goes:

I miss you and I'm sorry.
I usually don't apologize to anybody.
Should've met you halfway.
Should've asked you to stay.
When you gave me the chance to leave,
should've said "only if you come with me."
I should've swallowed my pride.

I was always happiest by your side.
It's all on me.
I'm the one to blame
and if you were here
I'd ask you to stay.
But you're in New York
and I said I'd leave that place.
But if you could answer my call,
I'll hope on a plane
and meet you at terminal eight.

I Would

If I could walk over water,
I'd be there in five.
If I could fly through space,
if I could turn back time,
I'd go back to the platform
where you nearly missed your flight
and tell you I'm not ready for goodbye.
Driving home alone,
the rain began to fall.
Couldn't tell if it was tragic
or hopelessly romantic
or some clichéd way
to help me through this storm.
If I could show up in Spain,
at least for a day,
because I find myself missing
how you'd burn all the pancakes
every single morning.
Oh, how I'd kill just to see your smile.
It's not the same through a phone
on a constantly lagging call
I can't wait for you to come home.
If only I could mail myself.
Tuck myself away
in the folds of a note.
I'll seal it up and stick it in a small envelope.
If only I could be with you.
Right now.
I call you at 3pm
but you miss it because, once again, I forget

we're fighting against time
and the clock isn't on our side.

Bullet Words

I was drunk,
it didn't mean a thing.
Just ignore
the bullets from my mouth.
The scars will heal.
Stop thinking about it.

Learned my lesson

That's what I get for believing in someone who looks like you.
Too beautiful.
Too good to me.
When will I learn?
Never trust the man
who's too good to be true.

Male-Minded Monologue

I hate the colour pink.
It seems frivolous.
It says I have no plans.
Glitter speaks of worse things.
A mental mess
full of cliched dresses.
You said I was different,
not like most,
you said it like a compliment.
I loved the way it sounded
until I resented
the way it sounded.

I love the colour pink.
I decorate my room with it
and dedicate it a whole day to celebrate
under the October full moon.
Be sure to call me a bitch
as I lead the boardroom.
Paint my eyes with glitter
spread it to my lips
so, when you tell me to smile
the one I form
will be a reflective glare.
Listen to the sound
of the heels
of every other girl
who I am exactly like.

Locker Room

A teenage dream
is just a naive girls fantasy.
The snake in the sequin dress
you promised the world to.
She broke your heart
and to you that's reason enough
to burn down every pink door front
you pass by on the street.
Shoot your toy gun
point blank at me.
Eliminate all consequence.
Judge, would you like to hear my defense
before throwing away the key
and taking him out for a beer?

What do you want from me?

I just wanted you to notice me --
to *see* me.
But you never did.
You only saw the fragments of me that everyone saw.
And when I'd tear down my wall;
show you more of me,
you'd shut your eyes,
turn your head,
and pretend like you couldn't see.
And then you'd call
asking why I disappeared
That's when I realized
You don't like me for me.
You like me for how I make you feel

A switch flipped in my mind
telling me I'll be just fine
if you never spoke to me again.
I don't care where you're going
or who you'll be with.
I stare at you reading
and I'm filled with discontentment.
But it wasn't all my fault.
You stopped caring too.
It was a mutual understanding
that we never liked each other to begin with
You were just tolerant
and I was taught to keep silent.

Between

I like the transitional seasons—
the in-between seasons.
Like autumn and spring.
It's when the world looks prettiest.

I like walking between buildings—
through alleys and pathways most don't know about.
Meeting the people who usually stay hidden.

I like staying between.
It's less extreme.
It's more personal.
And in this world,
we could all use a little more personal...
Don't you think?

Wish I'd Been Braver

He's been hurt too many times before.
I couldn't add to that pain.
I didn't want to add to the scar tissue
embedded in his heart.
Didn't want to add
to the callouses forever on his hands.
Couldn't add
to the strain in his eyes.
And the permanent tear streaks
that graze his face.
So, I watched him with others
and saw how they hurt him,
how they made him ache.
And as I wiped the tears from his face
I realized
I should have been braver
and I hurt him all along
by letting him go back to those who hurt him.
But isn't there some saying
about old habits dying?
I guess this was another phase
like biting my nails
and picking at my face.
Sorry you had to find yourself
in the crossfires.

Happy Birthday

I'll meet you down by the old train tracks.
We'll sit and watch them pass by
feel the wind on your face
drying your tired eyes.

Ode to the Beats.

For we were merely false hopes
walking in the footsteps of the greats.
And, for a moment there,
we were one of them.
We soared high
and spoke in forbidden tongues.
We read ancient books
as we sat in the darkest of corners.
And we held hands
as we stood on the ledge
and jumped into the endless possibilities
paved by those before us.
Singing a song of death,
of hope,
of new beginnings.
As we fell to the earth below us
only to be caught by wondrous winds
and fly towards the stars.
Humming our song of new beginnings,
of hope,
of death.

Ghost of you

Same blue eyes.
Same white smile.
Same red lips
you wore all the time.
But there's just something different here.
You still hold my hand
but not as tight.
Still wear the shirt
I gave you that night.
But the sleeves are worn,
the thread is torn.
We're not the same people we were.
You're just a reflection of the girl.
I don't know you anymore.
But I'm just too scared to let you go.
So please stay
here with me.
In this empty
apartment we used to call home.
Please stay
in my arms.
We're both too stubborn to admit
we would rather be apart.
So, say
those three words.
The ones we promised to each other
the ones we haven't returned
in forever.
Don't let me go.
For tonight let's pretend

we don't see how we hurt.
For tonight let's pretend
we don't see how much we yearn.
For tonight let's pretend
we'd rather be here.
For tonight let's pretend
you don't miss her perfume.
For tonight let's pretend
you don't miss her
the way I miss you.

Make me

In the palm of your hands, I rest.
A puppet, you control me.
With the slightest flick
of my bleeding string
you hold the answers to me.
Leave me in a box
to collect the dust.
I only ever aim to please.
All I ask, is you sew me back
after your dog is done chewing through me.

Spilled Wine

You made me hate Harry Styles.
Can't listen to Canyon Moon without crying
I can't hear Woman
without feeling bad for women
because you made me hate women
because you always talked to other women
then said you didn't care for other women.

Didn't Treat [me] With Kindness.
False love gave me blindness.
Instead made me put up with your bullshit.
I was left stranded In The Hallway
wondering where you disappeared to.
You ran off to New York
to be with another Woman
and you called her your baby.
Said her Sunflower eyes drove you crazy.

But then you came home.
Told me you were home.
Told me she meant nothing
but then you called to her in your sleep.
The Ghost of you in a dream.

Woke up the next morning.
Packed your bags the next morning.
I was Falling the next morning.
I was Lonely the next morning.
You left your record the next morning
and I played our song.

A sad song hidden in a happy mirage.
I should've known
you weren't as open as you told.

Kissed by a shadow

We were going 105 on the 401.
You didn't look ahead but instead at me.
In the passenger seat, I was staring ahead.
Your hands weren't even on the wheel.
I was a good girl,
a small-town beloved
and you were
quite the opposite.
We didn't fit
yet we did so perfectly.
You brought out the Gemini of me.

The sun set to the north of us
but I was staring at you.
A star filled sky
highlighted your birds eye view.
An omnipotent being,
you seemed to know it all.
That's when I realized,
I was beginning to fall.

The Cheshire moon
seemed to highlight your past mistakes
but I stuck close to the shade.
That's when I wanted you and me.
That's when we crashed into an apple tree.
The nest fell down, the birds flew away.
If only I'd listened
to what they had to say.

Red and blue lights wash you out.
Your cigarette eyes were the last thing I saw
before you walked away.
Kickstarted our final draw.
Swords out glistened under the wildfire,
burning me like a clipped wire.

I'm still sitting there.
Dust collecting in my idle stare.
Wheeled out by a stranger.
You were my first and final
brush with fate.
Maybe God decided against my good faith.

Would you be my rival?

Loving you is a game I play
as I pull the dagger away.
Throat turned red, we're the opposites
but they say we opposites attract.
Love is a battle, want to play?
Standing still under firelight
you realize nothing is as it seems.
Wake up realizing
it was all but a seemingly marvelous dream.

Leo Rising

And I know you used me
since the day we met
but I'm selfish
and I liked the attention
so, I didn't really mind at all.

Heartache

Break my heart and shatter my soul.
Eat me alive, don't let me go.
To walk on eggshells
beats walking on cobblestones.
Fight me in public,
use my name as a curse.
Tear me apart
and wreak a havoc I yearn.

Noah

Promise me
you won't become
a figment of my imagination.
An illusion I fail to recognize
even as you speak to me.
Please don't become
someone I cannot recall,
a memory I can't place,
a pigment I no longer see.

not my ideal storyline

Who would have known
I would have fallen
for the brown-eyed boy
with the crooked smile?
Lost his favourite ring
last week when he was stumbling
on his way to my house
when he replayed
the end of my favourite film.
Bought my love at the summer fair.
On top of the wheel,
we flew in the air.
Held onto reality with the tips of our fingers.
Oh, how that summer breeze lingered
in your curly brown hair
that September night.
Sounds of the lawnmower
played the song of our life.

Wrote It Down In Ink

I'll admit, I think you're
an arrogant son-of-a-bitch
wish you knew
more of what I was thinking.
You're not my baby, I know.
I just want to know the reason.
The reason why you left me
and why you stopped to care.
The reason you don't call me.
I think it's only fair.
I wrote you 365 letters
but you never wrote back.
Was this a story for the ages
or only for a moment
to take up some blank pages
until we could no longer speak?
I just wish you knew how it felt
to be sitting in this empty house
wish you'd know how it feels
to be this lonely.

Peach

I hate smoking
so, I bought the cheapest pack of cigarettes.
Now your drunk ramblings
are starting to make sense.
I don't know what you're saying
but I keep on listening.
Because you've got a pretty face
and I've been pretty lonely.

You got wasted
like all the potential I've been told I lack.
Walk out the bar holding your hand.
And as we leave, I notice your friends stare
usually that would bother me
but tonight, I don't care.
Because I'm tired of sleeping in a lonely bed.
and they've got pretty faces
and some prettier meds.

I hate the taste of smoke on your breath
but the way you say my name makes me forget.
Made my knees go weak as you ran your fingertips
down my spine
and I couldn't remember the name of the guy.
The one who broke my heart just last night.
The one I came to you for in the first place.
But now I can barely picture his face.
And I used to call him baby but not anymore
I think it suits you more
and if he's angry about it, all the better.

He should have treated me better.
Should have been better.
But you're better.

Just Tonight

Bright blue lights
on your hazel eyes.
I'm enchanted
just by the sight.
Can feel your hands
in my jeans,
If I say: "yes,
would you please"
just promise not to break me.

Run my fingers through your hair
I know they can see us
but I don't care.
Just stay beside me whispering
sweet nothings and promises of tomorrow.

As we stumble walking home
I just want to let you know
I may not love you for tomorrow
but tonight
you're my knight in shining armour.

Death by a Broken Love Song

I look out the window
at darkened skies.
Dull stars
that don't shine as bright.
So I kiss some stranger by the back door.
Feel nothing.
It's exactly what I'm looking for.
Stumble home;
it's 2am.
Don't ever want to go out again.
I see your face in everyone.
I go online,
see you're with the girl
you said I should trust.
Look in the mirror
all I see is you.
My hips marked by your tattoos.
My hands, my heart, my soul
all of it touched
you still chose
to walk out the door.
My eyes,
all they see is you.
My neck,
stained by your favourite perfume.

- J

Once upon a time
started with the last line
didn't say goodbye
should've turned around first
but I just had too much pride.
I should've taken my time,
rehearsed the lines,
counted to ten
before falling to my knees
and praying you would catch me
as I fell
down in tears
wishing you could only see
the spaces between the lines
of the broken promises
that died with a kiss goodnight.
Wish I had another try
maybe then you could hear
all I wanted to say.
But I took a step,
you raised your voice,
drowned under all the noise
and I laid down
and counted to ten.
Closed my eyes,
stepped into the bright lights.
Maybe one day
we'll give it another try.

Should've seen the signs,

rewrote the lines.
Wrong place, worst times.
Pieces of my peace of mind
stuck between the lines
all the times you didn't try.
Maybe words are better left unsaid
like the words "I love you" bolded in red.
Words I could never say,
maybe they'll come eventually
or maybe I'll rest trying to find the peace
you claimed to give me.

Peter

We were playing hide and seek.
It's getting hard to breathe.
Please give me a reason.
I knew you
tried to rewrite all the endings
and pass them off as true
and they all believed you.
You said Tinkerbell died of a natural cause.
As though Peter didn't leave her
bruised and scarred.
Told them Wendy left
out of her own free will.
Left out the part
where she was almost killed.
I knew you
like the back of my hand.
Told me you
would always try to understand.
I knew you,
or at least I thought I did.
Until you left me to drown
in a vat of acid.
I knew you
kept trying to rewrite the endings.
Told me great life happens
while you're busy making plans.
But I didn't know
you were leaving me to die.
Planned my death.
Looked for me to cry.

As you bury me in this sunken hole.
All I wanted was to sit front row.
Maybe I should have just listened to Hook
when he told me to strike,
said, "take another look.
At those deep green eyes
you fell so hard for."
A pirate could have been
something worth the dying for.

Hoax

Blue was the colour of my dress
the night you told me this wasn't working.
Funny enough,
that was the first night I told you
I loved you.
Looks like I needed to lose you
to want you.
And I'm sorry for the pain I caused
I'm sorry I strung you along
But can you blame me
I was only seventeen.

Now blue is the colour I avoid
I associate it with a bad choice.
But it's fine
never really liked it all that much.
Surely, you've moved
but I still wonder, when you hear that song
the one we danced to all summer long
do you think of me
or turn it off?
And if I showed up at your doorstep
Would you recognize the girl
who broke your heart?
or would you slam the door in her face?
But can you really blame me?
I'm only 21.

Clandestine

Please don't call me your baby anymore.
You lost that title a long time ago.
The day you told her to get in your car,
then you snuck out together
to the back of the bar.
And don't call me your girl.
Not anymore
I don't want to be the girl
You crushed by the back door.

Autumn leaves fall down
like pieces into a too tight place.
You told me it was an August fling
but I was there in September
when she pulled up
and told you to get in.
I was there in December
when you turned your phone
face down.
I should've put my foot down.
I shouldn't have put myself down.
I should've walked out
but the February air was icy
and your sweater kept me warm.
Smelling of her perfume.
right before the night
I told you I knew.

But I guess that's what happens
when you finally notice

longing stares
and illicit affairs,
stolen kisses
and a light touch
on the arm you used to wrap around
the one you claimed you loved.
Trusted the one
left in the dust.

So, when you see my face
in a crowded room
tell me does she smile
since she found the truth
or does she scream?
Does she choke on the lies
you fed her almost every night?
Does she crumble into the earth
so that you can laugh without feeling hurt?

Tell me, did you tell her the truth
when you met me then
told me you had to go home?
Did you let her know I was waiting for you
when you gave her that ring
that Thursday afternoon?
Did you tell her it was a gift from me to you?
Did you tell her about that very first night
by the fireside you let me see you cry?
Did you mention your parents love
and how they lacked all that we made up?
Or did you mirror those same words to me
I guess a mirror's all we'll ever be.

Sabaism

Turns out, the answer
to what happens when
an optimist
and an acosmist
meet, is us.
The destruction
to our perfectly chaotic story
stained with spilled coffee
and drops of ink
illegibly trying to reassemble
at the cost of nothing but
trembling hands,
black-stained tears,
and a quiver in every breath.
Tucked away is the
worn journal,
collecting dust,
stained red papercuts
deliriously elated
under false pretense.
The full moon
brings out the creatures of the night,
that's what grandma always said.
Stick to the road, little red,
on your way home.
But your honeyed fields
called my name.

RSVP: Declined

Cancelling plans just in case you called.
Blowing off friends just in case you called.
Waiting alone on a Friday night
as all my friends go out
living their lives.

But he didn't call.
She stayed in bed refreshing her phone.
Stop staying at home.
Let's go to the movies,
to our favourite spot downtown.
But she said she can't.
Plans three weeks in the making,
but she would rather cancel and stay home.
"James is off from work."
So, she put on her highest heels
and her shortest miniskirt.

Then I went out
with all of our friends.
Walked back home
around 2am.
Passed by her house.
She was sitting on the front porch
crying on the phone.
"You told me you were coming
what happened to you."
He told her he was with some friends,
"but thinking of you."
James said they could go out now,

if she'd like.
As I locked my doors,
I saw headlights
shining down the block.
Pulling in with a loud song.
She hates that band
and everyone knows
but she gets in the car
adjusting her clothes.
Shoots me a quick text to cancel the day's plans.
"Sorry he just texted.
He wants to take me out again."

What she won't see

Every day I watch her
succumb for a love
that vibrates the walls
and creates static through the phone.
Every day I watch her
sink over swim
and crawl into a ball
for a love
who's boots break the floorboards.
Her life is mastered
by palinoia
for a love
I can hear from her.
By a love
she hides me from
because God forbid
I give her a word
to describe her love
that better fits.

10:18

The end of a new age
hit with all it's might
as though the sun rise
marked the start of a new film.
The supporting cast was fired.
Turns out the audience wasn't a fan
of the age-old best friend.
who lost herself to a man.
Souls forgotten.
Switched roles with a doormat.
Tattered around the edges.
A Gemini's defences.
No lines to memorize.
Refusing to ask for more.
She felt this was her next
award-winning role.

22

The confetti sticks to the walls
and the glitter drips down
like acid tears on my pillowcase
ripped from the pillow fight.

My high heel broke in half
climbing on the table.
I looked down
and didn't see you around.

Mascara smudges under my eyes
from sweat, tears, or the hours passed
I cannot decide.

I left my phone under
my mattress at home
hoping for a missed call
that would never show.

One more smile in
the bathroom mirror.
There's a line outside
of friends wanting to take pictures
in this reflective frame I'm falling into.
I thought the one thing I could commit to
would be here.
That's what you said
but then they
showed up and you ran.

Inhaled the helium.
Lightheaded was the way to go.
Lose control
in this empty house.
Locked in a room.
Cake bound.
Though, it was made for two,
you weren't around.
He clouded your point of view.
Final line, he made you cross.
I guess I was wrong about you.
I guess controlling was the side you chose.
I guess you really fell for his cologne
standing on the other side of the door.
I froze, you ran
to catch the man
you'd later cry about.

Phones go both ways

What do you do
when the only thing you notice in a crowded room
is the only one who didn't show?
Broken promises discarded on my bedroom floor.
Guess it isn't a bliss to fill with arrogance.

This is Why We Can't Have Nice Things

I miss screaming so loud
we drown out the thunder.
Miss crying in the rain;
being in a constant state of wonder.
I don't want to know what's happening next.
Don't want you to be my new best friend.
I miss sitting by the phone
waiting for your call.
Then leaving because I got bored.
2am we have a loving brawl.
Tired of predictability.
I'd rather a "screw you"
being screamed at me.
Come out to my window,
throw your things in the pool.
Pull myself a Daisy.
Think Carraway would be proud of you?
Shoot me dead,
bury me in riches,
call my friends
a wild pack of bitches
who you think influence me poorly.
But I don't care.
At least it's not boring.

Late night phone call

Called me, woke me up again
from my restful sleep. It's 2am.
There has to be a root
for your narcissism—
your egotistical,
dysfunctional,
colloquialisms.
I'll be right here
if you ever need me
but please don't ever need me.
Maybe try some medication.
Maybe try some isolation
with your thoughts
and figure out
why you push your distress
onto everyone else
and let me go back to sleep.

Sincerely,
I'm no longer yours to keep.

same name

The story begins last September in a crowded room.
We were snug together
breathing in some girl's perfume.
Saw you standing in the corner
a new face, never seen before.
Shot me a smile,
instantly knew I wanted more.

Next chapter, we see
texts between you and me
but you were overseas
so that's all they'd ever be.
Just a cluster of electrons
floating through space
filled with you missing me
and wanting me in your grace.
I mean, I guess you were cute.
Seemed like a fine time.
Begging me to come visit
after every line.
Told me about a dream you had
where I jumped on a plane
on my way to see you.
Said you'd show me around—
take me to your favourite place.

Chapter three we set the scene:
we're still on opposite sides of the globe
breathing in pieces of fabric.
I slowly forget the smell of your cologne.

Two weeks later,
hadn't heard from you
but it looks like you found
a new favourite perfume
dressed up in a jewel
that costs more than my apartment.
The one you never got to see.
In a ruby red gown,
hand placed where your heart is.

Last chapter is where
out to you, I no longer reach.
Talk to my friends
about the boy who begged for me.
Last chapter is where
you no longer get to see me.
Finally, we reach
the end of our story.

Thank You, Anxiety

Thank you, anxiety
for giving me a reason to stay in bed all day.
Shoutout to the lack of dopamine
for telling me I'm crazy
as I waste my days away.
Here's a toast to the feeling of panic
that disables me to sleep.
Thank you, for making me hate me.

Thank you, anxiety
for telling me I suck
at every hour of the day.
Thank you to trepidation
for telling me I'm going to die
at every second of the day.
Raise a glass to the feeling of dread
that washes over me.
Thank you to my brain
for keeping me in misery.
I can always count on your consistency.

Thank you, anxiety
for giving me nothing
besides debt by therapy.
Thank you, anxiety
for giving me the worst of me
I can always count on you.
Thank you
...I lose.

Act V

You made me hate my favourite band.
Spoke to the King of Capulet
and said I was your Juliet.
I should've known
we live a masquerade.
I should've known
to never fight with fate.
Mamma told me
keep my windows closed.
I should've known.
Should've listened to Rosaline.
Sat on the side of the dance
away from you all night.
I should've left sooner.
With a dagger, cut through.
Bless thy apothecary
aid in my undoing.

Thought I Could Change

You have a way
of coming in with the rain
on a seemingly sunny day.
So, I start another fight
my breath fogs up the glass
because, once again,
I'm screaming to my rear-viewed past.
Kidding myself, I say
this time will be different,
you're all I want.
But you can't be what I wanted.
Hold myself back for as long as I can.
You tap on my door
and I'm back to yearning.

Dance with me to the beat of thunder
and glow in the headlights
as I fall in love with the lightening.

Thursday Night Musings

Sit still
look pretty
curly hair won't do it, honey.
Burn it straight.
Fill your lips.
Plastic tastes like candy cane.
Brows too thick
pluck them thin.
Who knew bigger brows were back in?
Sit up straight.
You're too tall.
I guess I'll see myself out the door.
It's a typical night
hating what I see
when I look in the mirror
and see the typical me.
What's a girl to do
besides drown in a bottle of pink perfume.

Can't wear a skirt,
my legs are too long.
Can't take one more detention,
five schools so far.
Rebecca made out
with my boyfriend last week.
We're both crying in the bathroom.
Happy Sweet Sixteen.
She likes girls,
she likes boys,
flipping through pages of a magazine

but she just can't be
so she dates the captain of the football team.

Sit in front of a screen
where no one looks like me.
Had coffee for breakfast
every day this week.
Too thin, too thick.
So contradictory.
No wonder I need some therapy.
Turn out the light,
crawl into bed.
What's a girl to do
but muse inside her head.

Alex

The age-old story of
boy-meets-boy,
that's what I said.
Crooked toothed laughter.
Quit playing pretend.
Too old for dress up games,
time to put the masque away.

It's the tired story of
mom and dad.
Cries and failures
pace in my head.
Drown out the noise,
bury me in my bed.
How do I say
I'm no different
then the golden boy,
that's what they called me.
Starlit palms
buried in my star-filled eyes.
Looks like the golden boy
is dying inside.
Lost in a black hole
below contempt.
He thought the answer
would be obvious.

It's the heart-warming lines
the I love you's.
But what happens when

they no longer love you too?
Thought my crash and burn
would be their last
but it looks like
the skater boy
meets golden boy
meets lost boy
meets broken boy
meets the trials of
an~~ un~~conditional love.

Do you remember
in the room to your right
at the end of the hall
we were playing card games
I was starting to fall
but I couldn't let you know yet.
It was my kept secret.

Then, time flies.
Messy as my mind.
Stained glass windows
blurred my heart. A sight
caused sore eyes.
Dog eared the pages
of my high-wired
hard times.

Deck the ivy-filled halls
we once knew.
Except this place is no longer
filled with memory.
Our spot no longer
waits for you and me.
Tear the pages out
of our burning story.
Lock the freshly painted room
at the end of the hall

Occupancy for two

Daisy

Dance in your linen shirts
strewn around your living room.
It only cost me
my whole life.

Jump in the swimming pool.
Living in a champagne flute.
You are a once in
a lifetime.

Choke on my bleached-white pearls.
Run away. Hiding from her.
It will just cost you
your green light.

Fall in your swimming pool.
Red wine stains. Eyes, silver hue.
Hope your view was worth
your gold tomb.

Absquatulate

I was looking for a reason,
so, I blamed it on the season.
Everything is different under snow.
Your diaphanous eyes let me know
how much you yearn—
how much you hurt.
But my ice-coloured glasses
filter out your damage,
helped pack my baggage
to whisk myself away
while you beg me to stay.

Daddy Issues

You told me I have sad eyes
leaning against the bricks.
Fell from his pedestal
onto your lips.
Looks like my madhouse
was built for two.
I was blinded by your eyes.
They blurred my view.
Your frenetic love
scarred my heart
but it burned so good.
The scabs are my least-favourite part.
The worst decision I ever made
was falling too late.
Because I'd rather be
slipping through Oz,
Mad Hatter's hand holding mine,
than be with you.
So, tell me why
you're the one I choose.

I Now Pronounce You

Match made in manipulation.
Heart chords held by annihilation.
Heavy as the hand that
crumbled me. Down I sank
to my knees.
Expected me to raise a toast
to the two who never loved me;
I don't think. Was I worth it?
What did you expect? More perfect?
If I sat up straighter
was a lady?
If I said yes
to the ring who broke me.

Gossamer

Isn't it funny how
the shape of your name
spells out pain,
each curve as sharp as a blade.
You left me stranded
in the afterglow
of your shadow.
I should've known.
Your eyes ardently frantic.
Calamities wasted.
Always kept frustrated.
Kept barefoot in your wildest winter.
My dirt-filled bed
feels so warm
in your plot.

Objections

Stood there
on the sidelines
wishing for a future
I'd never hold.
Sat in the pews
of a memory
I must let go.
The warm light
of the open
refrigerator door
was out like
a power chord
with the dullest blade
I had ever seen.
Please tell me sometimes
you wish it were me
who had said alright
that September night.
Am I still
in your wallet
beside the ring
that you stored
for her?
Shouldn't have said no.
Do you wish
it were me still
to call you a contrarian
while you yell
I'm pretentious,
enigmatic,

hopelessly tragic?
In a black dress
I mourn
a life I never
came to know.
In a white dress
I mourn
a life I never
wanted to hold.

عزرائیل

For I am in love with death.
Every evening
he picks me up
and we run away
to a far-off place.
As I lie awake
I wait for the day
he decides to, forever,
whisk me away.
For all I want
is to be near him—
to be protected
under his cloak
and shielded
from my troubles.

End of Days

Pluck the golden apple
from the tree
and feast on its juices.
Let the golden leaves
tickle your cheeks
as you moan in a hum
at the sweetness they provide,
filling you deep inside.
So, come with me
and you will see
the Garden of Eden
is where we shall reside.

Precipice

Your touch
lingers against my scars.
You had the nerve
to call me yours.
Rang the bell to my madness
broke the lock to my madhouse—
to a cavern
of solace.
Crept in my cavity
to live out
a Sisyphus fantasy.
Chisel down my heart of stone
mould it into something more.
Break through my crystal view.
Crystalize this Valentine.
I hope I never see you soon.

Stockholm Syndrome

You are an expert at "no."
Valuing my "yes."
Like a moth to a flame
you keep my dungeon warm.
But the spark ignited
my settling shivers.
Tie each bracelet you gave
tightly around each wrist.
Pulsating against the steel
are my transparent veins.
The flame you give
will melt the ice away.
So long as I stay still
in the impact of your hurricane.

Inconsequential

I could write about love;
a feeling I cannot express—
through refusal or inability
I will not confess.
I could rip up this page.
But if you asked what is wrong,
I'd fall mute. Unable to profess
the pouring rain
I hold in my heart.
I could stain this page
with some cheap ink
and a few quick strokes
of my jewel-adorned wrist
but these futile devices
are just that.
I guess in this life,
love is something
I am meant to lack.

Plot Points

What happens if the bad guy is the good guy?
What if the good guy is a wicked in disguise?
What if story books were all a lie?
What if true love's kiss led to the kill?
What if all my will led to the death brigade
I've created for myself?
For I am all I can count on.
Especially for matters as sensitive as this.

Evermore

For through the darling whims
and my careless musings.
Through my unkempt childlike ways
and my lonesome gaze.
You stuck through it all,
sat on the grass
in the sunlit bath
over the grave of life.
I lay
searching for a pulse
in your lingering sense
against my fingertips.
Feeding me breath
through photosynthesis.
You are the golden light
I hid from.
Only roaming the dark.
Yet, you rose every morning
keeping me from falling apart.

Midnight

Why is it that
when the moon goes up,
suddenly I go down?
I crash and I burn
and I ask myself why.
My friends are fine,
my heart's not broken,
and my family no longer fights.
Yet I feel this forlorn
effluence of pressure
on my chest
that disappears around 12pm.
It lulls me to sleep
like the weighted blanket
I refuse to purchase
because why would I buy
added pressure
when I can make my own
out of absence.

Tortured artist

Ever since
I was little
I was obsessed
with the idea of
suffering.
I thought that's what
I'm meant to do.
Cut off a limb or two.
Stick my head
in an appliance.
That's what all
the pretty girls do
in every film I see
Growing up,
tragedy was
everything.
So, light me up
from within.
Tear through my
broken skin.
Bleed me out of my sin.
Choke me
on the pills
I try not to swallow.
Are you done with your happiness?
Is it something I could borrow?
All the pretty girls in film
rim their eyes with black ink,
cover up their accent
pieces of their bliss.

So, don't catch me when I fall.
The concrete
is the warmest bed of them all.
Lock me up in the highest tower,
dare me not to jump
for the tragedy
was always my
favourite part.
Kiss my lips with poison.
Stab me in the heart
you ripped out from my chest
with your bare hands.
Lay me down to rest
just for eternity.
Shower me with wishes
of tranquility.
The tragedy was
always my
favourite part.
The tragedy
is where I
wish I could start.

Holding on to healing

I am Salinger in the woods
contemplating my mild existence.
Wordsworth calls to me,
musing tempestuously.

To assassinate my hero's.

Let their words speak through me.
Let my tongue change their speech.

Alcott cries
through my mind,
whispering words of hopeful lies.
Dickinson scratches the walls of me.
Death lingers,
a dear friend of mine.

To rot with my hero's.

Let their ink stain my soul.

Darwish argues with Bukowski's prose.

Drown in the drink of my hero's.

My blind optimism
stabbed with pens.
My veins bleed out their ink
as I chant, "again."

Pass the time

They say if you can't sleep
try counting some sheep.
But what do I do if the sheep don't show up?
What do I do if I want to throw up
from laying in my bed?
Empty thoughts run through my head.
Staring at a wall,
I feel like I may fall
into an abyss
full of nothingness
and I count back by ten.
The numbers mix in my head
so I stare at the ceiling fan
wishing I was leant a hand.
A guiding figure
to guide me from my distress.
So, I lay in bed awake
thinking I'm a big mistake.
I make up false scenarios
hoping that's how my life could go.
Count back by threes,
I relive the miseries
I thought I forgot about.
Maybe I could live without
counting sheep,
losing sleep.
Fictitious thoughts in my head
only arrive once I'm in bed.
I begin to count the stars instead.

Across the lake

They're all tired of
hearing about daisy.
That cruel flower
makes them go crazy.
She'll spill your blood
and wipe it away
With her million-dollar coat train.
Laugh at the others,
they must be fools.
They just linger.
But she has you
basking in her glory
for your whole life.
Too scared to make her
your one true wife.
She sits on the pedestal
you carved out
specially made
for Her cruel lady.
Lady, lady that sweet daisy.

But I'm a Nice Guy

Baby, you don't need me.
What you need is therapy
I can't stay up all night with you
analyzing your issues.
You say you can't be tied down
but always want me around.
I'm not your therapist.
You're just a sad masochist.

I can't be your girlfriend,
I can't promise you the end.
You say all you want is me
but whenever we get close you disappear.
I'm not asking you to choose,
it's just that I'm left confused.
You push and pull with no remorse
and I'm left a mat at your front door.

I can't help you fix you.
Stop dragging me into your issues.
I try to lend a friendly ear,
yet what you hear is "fuck me."
I'm done with all the games you play.
Fix yourself and call me one day.
I can't be your therapist.
I've reached the end of it.

Pray

As I lay my head to rest
these soft words, I do know best
escape my lips in detriment.
I pray tonight I shall finally win.
I pray this will be my final sink.
I pray for an eternal rest.
Maybe in damnation, I will be content.

Lock the Door

The highs were lower
than the abyss I call home.
Every day I kid myself
and say this time is different.
But each day I crawl
in the hole I call a home
and make-believe
with the pretty monster hidden
beneath my bed.
The pretty monster crawls
into my head.
She sounds like me.
She acts it too.
The manic induced sadness
is warmer than you.

Fairy Tale Dreaming

The blue bird was lost
helping Cinderella.
It felt the tatter
of its tired wings.
So, it flew away
in search of Juliet.
Too late, for she
met with a corpse
in the shiniest tomb.
Made a quick escape,
away from the city.
The blue bird found solace
on a shiny spindle
of the golden spinning wheel.
Staring longingly at Aurora,
the blue bird made friends
with the black crow.
Death and fragmented wings
are now the prettiest sight
the little blue bird
ever did see.

You're an Oil Painting

Footsteps in fresh snow.
Your ivy leaves
wrapped around my throat.
Lost in the cracked lights.
Slipped on black ice.
Teardrops frozen to my face.
I thought it was a wonderful time
but coal burned down our house.
You took the reins and crashed the sleigh.
My dismembered love
dizzy in my snow globe
full of desired flakes.

Serpent

Dear Athena, shall I pray unto thee.
All you need, an affair I shall conceive.
Punish my sacrilegious behaviour
I will gladly repent my serpent way
if thou allows a rightful punishment.

Paramour

You wake up and brush through your hair
to meet a man with a back-alley stare.
A million other wives for a one-night affair.
Your favourite skirt, torn with care,

placed upon the pillow by your head.
You plead for one night of rest.
Taste the hand that presses to your chest.
Don't talk to strangers, a wise man once said,

but he did not know the one before you.
On your knees, you show gratitude.
Louder than words do actions speak.
The only kind words you've heard in weeks

was the loving tug of your mangled tresses.
Watch girls walk by in their little sundresses.

For no perfume would smell as sweet
as the tangled bedsheets of last week.

The breakup isn't the worst part

It's the part before.
The "I know it's over"
before it's officially over.
The cry yourself to sleep
because you can tell what's here.
You know what's coming.
The anticipation before the crash
into the sharp rocks
you didn't notice in the fall.

Detect a Language

To be lost in translation
of the stories of our lives
so I could tell you everything
without saying anything
and be free.

Bookstore Boy

The rays of light
favoured your face
on this bleak winter day.
Though our fingers touched
for less than a moment
already, I was dreaming
of whisperings in bookshelves.
It should have taken two minutes,
this transaction of ours,
but your deep-set eyes
had other plans in mind.
Your lips formed the sounds
of questions you knew,
the signs around held all the answers to you.
Five minutes later,
three more cashiers were called up
working on a line
that wasn't there before.
Then I called my friends
and told them about the bookstore boy
that gave minimum wage worth.

Across the Street

The boy with the brown eyes
doesn't let anyone near.
As if vulnerability
is a life or death fear.
My mother, I try to convince.
She doesn't know
who the man beneath is.

Hidden behind quick remarks
and surly smiles.
The one who rarely talks.
The one who speaks of Hemmingway
and Shakespeare in the Park.
He sends me classic tales of Poe
and playlists with my name
when he knows I cannot rest.
Under the full moon, I lay
and wait for the three rings
of my battered phone,
to hear him speak in a barely-there whisper.
The angels shan't hear
the trouble he gotten into.

Forlorn and frightened
are the descriptors used
when I file the report
for a missing muse.
Who took a trip across the country
and never told a soul.
So, I spend my days

wishing for an unknown caller,
an unidentified voice,
that could possibly be
from the saddest boy.

1969 AMC

Sad boy with the sad eyes
trading sly smiles
across deserted ballrooms
in a December light.
Was it a lie?
Or was it the one moment
of true honesty.
Fragile hostility.
Toxic vulnerability.
You said make a wish
under the New York sky
and kiss the stars
a fair goodnight.
Setting my time
to the return
of my sanity.
Return of my dignity.
All pride left
that faithless night
of stop signs glittered with headlights.

Mid-June

It's been months,
though it feels like years,
since I've seen your twinkle-light smile
and worn your October night palms
or stared into your apple cider eyes
and traced your pumpkin spiced lips.
I thought time healed all wounds
but it seems, like secrets,
I would have to die
for the cliche to be true.
And I just might.
For missing you
is the hardest thing
I've ever had to do.

My favourite accessory is your hand

What doesn't kill you
only makes you stronger
but I'd rather kill myself
than go through this again.
After all, I am my mother's daughter.
If he doesn't kill you,
he can take it to the end.
So, I'll mind my tongue.
Bite my business.
Staple your mouth shut,
sew your eyes open.
Asleep in the tree
of 333 Hades Street.
Drink my champagne tears
gone stale from spilling
and sticking to the spiderwebs.
Waiting for when I lay in the dirt.
Shall you cry after me
shouting a Pompeii ballad.

Drank too much

He loves the smell of cigarettes
but only when he's drunk.
And he likes how it feels when his hair's wet
after the pouring rain's gone dry.
But he can't stand the taste of his mouth
when he's gone too far.
And he hates the feeling in his heart
that tells his he feels too much.
So, he listens
to the world.
And he listens
to her
when she tells him
she hates the taste of his mouth
after he drinks too much.

He hates the smell of smoke
and how the world is burning down.
And he hates the sound of a car horn
after someone's wandered too far out.
And he hates the feeling of being alone
in this too-crowded small town.
And that's why he drowns it out with smoke
and drinks until he drowns.

Miss Your Mirage

I miss a boy I've never met.
I miss the "goodnight" texts you never sent.
I miss the arm you never wrapped around me.

I miss the hand you never held.
I miss the look you never gave.
I miss the feeling you could never generate
that followed the "I love you" that never came.

I miss the boy you never were.
Miss the words I never heard.
Miss the you that was never there.

Miss the you that, turns out, never cared.

Seven Levels

You probably told her you're lonely,
that you don't know what to do with yourself.
And you're probably saying
all these pretty words,
the ones you save
for the pretty girls.
But don't tell her forever,
forever means nothing from your mouth.
My eyes may be like the earth
but hers are the sky
and the oceans too.
Though I may not burn,
red always looked good on you.

برزخ

When I sleep
I am finally free.
My soul can go back to the place
it chose to leave.
Betraying me
instead of staying put.
In the land of spirits
is where I'd like to go.

but where are you *really* from?

I'm a pretty girl
but only in comparison.
I'm a smart girl
but only when away from him.

You think she's my sister
told you I only have a brother
but said the fabric on our heads
made us look identical.
So much that you forgot.
Her blue eyes rolled
and with a tired sigh,
my brown ones closed.

Said you didn't know "someone of my kind"
could be so damn beautiful.
Said "Amen" 'cause Christianity's
the only one with your approval.

Told me my clothes were too tight;
what would God think.
But then called me a prude
when I wouldn't suck your dick.

Said he's never been
with a Muslim girl before
asked if we could hook up
like a bucket list score.

Called me golden

said I was glowing.
Like the sand from the desert
I must've resided in.

Said I was cute
said I was quite
but, honey, you have no clue
of the fire igniting.

If I'm not from here
then neither are you
because this land was stolen
so even though you were also born here
with your logic, I guess you must be an "immigrant"
too.

In loving memory of

I heard it's in poor taste
to eulogize someone
as they stand there breathing.
I heard it's ill-mannered
to bury someone
before they finish bleeding.

Garden of Eden

To be a rose
adrift in the wind
with a thorn to prick
the troubles lurking.
By the prick of one's finger
may stories arise.
In the bouquet of Lady Macbeth,
crush my petals dry
into a fine powder
to make a strong tea.
Take down the king
of All Hallows' eve.
To be thy saviour.
Thy dark shallow knight.
I bid thee
a final goodnight.

INDEX

Tragedies	5
Care for an adventure?	6
Mizpah	7
Ketamine	8
First Time	9
Nervous	10
Didn't think people like you still existed.	11
The Secret History	12
Up 'til 3am	13
Something about you	14
Dance with me	15
You Are My Home	16
Blank	17
What I Want	18
Do You Like Me?	19
I Choose You.	20
Van Gogh's Got Nothing on You	21

Meet me at the overpass.	22
Shine for You	23
truly, madly, deeply	24
They asked me about love.	25
Up at Night	26
How don't you know?	27
Since We Were Kids	28
Can we try again?	30
A Play Worthy Kind of Love	31
I Like Me Better with You	32
exhale	33
Roses are red, Vol. 1	35
Roses are red, Vol. 2	36
He	37
My Favourite Virus	38
Back to November	39
Hey...	40
Solstice	41

Fairy Lights	42
Darkest Winter	43
It's the most wonderful time of the year	44
92 Johnson Avenue	47
Lily	49
You asked me what my problem was...	50
Miss You	51
Your Weather Report	53
'tis the season	54
Don't love you but I can't be alone right now	55
u up?	57
Miss Misfortune	59
Hades	60
Crow	61
you asked me not to be scared	62
Prince of Hell	63
Calling Aphrodite	65
He looks as pretty as the Devil	66

Cecilia	67
Wish you would	68
Reboot	69
Climate change	70
Legend Says	71
eulogize me to the songs of Sinatra	73
Remind me why I left	74
I Would	76
Bullet Words	78
Learned my lesson	79
Male-Minded Monologue	80
Locker Room	81
What do you want from me?	82
Between	83
Wish I'd Been Braver	84
Happy Birthday	85
Ode to the Beats.	86
Ghost of you	87

Make me	89
Spilled Wine	90
Kissed by a shadow	92
Would you be my rival?	94
Leo Rising	95
Heartache	96
Noah	97
not my ideal storyline	98
Wrote It Down In Ink	99
Peach	100
Just Tonight	102
Death by a Broken Love Song	103
- J	104
Peter	106
Hoax	108
Clandestine	109
Sabaism	111
RSVP: Declined	112

What she won't see	114
10:18	115
22	116
Phones go both ways	118
This is Why We Can't Have Nice Things	119
Late night phone call	120
same name	121
Thank You, Anxiety	123
Act V	124
Thought I Could Change	125
Thursday Night Musings	126
Alex	128
Occupancy for two	130
Daisy	131
Absquatulate	132
Daddy Issues	133
I Now Pronounce You	134
Gossamer	135

Objections	136
عزرائیل	138
End of Days	139
Precipice	140
Stockholm Syndrome	141
Inconsequential	142
Plot Points	143
Evermore	144
Midnight	145
Tortured artist	146
Holding on to healing	148
Pass the time	149
Across the lake	150
But I'm a Nice Guy	151
Pray	152
Lock the Door	153
Fairy Tale Dreaming	154
You're an Oil Painting	155

Serpent	156
Paramour	157
The breakup isn't the worst part	158
Detect a Language	159
Bookstore Boy	160
Across the Street	161
1969 AMC	163
Mid-June	164
My favourite accessory is your hand	165
Drank too much	166
Miss Your Mirage	167
Seven Levels	168
برزخ	169
but where are you *really* from?	170
In loving memory of	172
Garden of Eden	173

ABOUT THE AUTHOR

Zeinab Fakih is a Lebanese-Canadian writer, poet and creator. Fakih has sought to create a dreamworld with her words for the lovers, romantics, and dreamers. Growing up with her nose in a book and a pen in her hand, it came as no surprise that she would one day write books of her very own.

Pulling inspiration from her personal adventures, her friends, and her imagination, she dug deep on her emotions and allows them to fuel her writing.

Visit http://thoughtsbyzeinab.weebly.com

www.ingramcontent.com/pod-product-compliance
Lightning Source LLC
Chambersburg PA
CBHW042236090526
44589CB00006B/73